D0560236

SONGS FROM HEAVEN

Tommy Walker
with Phil Kassel

Regal

From Gospel Light
Ventura, California, U.S.A.

Regal

PUBLISHED BY REGAL BOOKS
FROM GOSPEL LIGHT
VENTURA, CALIFORNIA, U.S.A.
PRINTED IN THE U.S.A.

Regal Books is a ministry of Gospel Light, a Christian publisher
dedicated to serving the local church. We believe God's vision
for Gospel Light is to provide church leaders with biblical,
user-friendly materials that will help them evangelize, disciple
and minister to children, youth and families.

It is our prayer that this Regal book will help you discover
biblical truth for your own life and help you meet the needs
of others. May God richly bless you.

*For a free catalog of resources from Regal Books/Gospel Light, please
call your Christian supplier or contact us at* 1-800-4-GOSPEL *or*
www.regalbooks.com.

Rights for publishing this book in other languages are
contracted by Gospel Light Worldwide, the international nonprofit
ministry of Gospel Light. Gospel Light Worldwide also provides
publishing and technical assistance to international publishers
dedicated to producing Sunday School and Vacation Bible School
curricula and books in the languages of the world. For additional
information, visit www.gospellightworldwide.org; write to
Gospel Light Worldwide, P.O. Box 3875, Ventura, CA 93006;
or send an e-mail to info@gospellightworldwide.org.

Regal revised version published July 2005
© 2001 Get Down Ministries
All rights reserved.

Library of Congress Cataloging-in-Publication Data
Walker, Tommy.
  Songs from heaven / Tommy Walker with Phil Kassel.
    p. cm.
  Includes bibliographical references.
  ISBN 0-8307-3783-9 (hardcover)
  1. God—Worship and love. 2. Praise of God. 3. Contemporary Christian music—Writing and publishing. I. Kassel, Phil. II. Title.

BV4817.W34 2005
782.25—dc22   2005013317

1 2 3 4 5 6 7 8 9 10 / 10 09 08 07 06 05

DEDICATION

THIS BOOK IS DEDICATED TO MY DAUGHTER,
EILEEN MARILYN MARIE WALKER—
I LOVE YOU SO MUCH. YOU ARE SUCH A
BEAUTIFUL, RADIANT BEAM OF
GOD'S GLORY. WHAT A GIFT YOU ARE
TO ME! I PRAY THAT YOU WILL BECOME
A PASSIONATE WORSHIPER OF GOD,
THE ONE WHO BROUGHT YOU
INTO THIS WORLD.

contents

acknowledgments

First, I would like to thank my mom, Eileen Walker. She is the first person to make me believe that I could ever write a song.

To my wife, Robin, for listening to me and supporting me long before there was any tangible reason to do so. To my pastor, Mark Pickerill, for doing the same.

To the worshiping congregation of Christian Assembly: Many of my songs are now heard around the world because you were so willing to try something new with such open hearts.

To my siblings and their friends, who surrounded me with such a creative atmosphere way back in the early '70s. To all my buddies with whom I played in Christian garage bands for all those years.

A huge thank-you to my friend Phil Kassel. Your many added words, thoughts, and countless hours on this project will never be fully known by most people, but I thank you from the bottom of my heart. Great job, my brother!

Finally, I'm so glad that I have this unique opportunity to tell the Lord, with so many witnesses, how much I thank Him for every song He has ever given me. Lord, I have experienced no greater joy in my life than to tell You how much I love You and then see others do the same. All this has been done through simple thoughts that You gave to me. Every melody, lyric and rhythm I've ever created has not only been *for* You, but it has been *from* You. What a gracious, generous, creative God You are! Thank You for letting me be a part of Your heavenly worship team here on Earth! All glory, honor and power to Your great name, Lord Jesus, both now and forevermore. Amen.

He put a new song in my mouth,
a hymn of praise to our God.
Many will see and fear and put
their trust in the Lord.

PSALM 40:3

I've been writing songs since I was 11 years old—longer than I've done anything else. Songwriting has become a completely natural part of my life, but not in the sense that every song I've written has been good. (I wrote songs for more than 15 years before I had any measure of what the world would consider success!) Songwriting is natural to me in the sense that from the beginning it has been a very fulfilling way to express love and worship to my God. Some of my early songs are very precious to me, and they were certainly necessary to get me ready to write songs for a larger audience.

My point is that every song that you write has merit, even if God is the only one who will ever hear it. Some songs are meant for just one moment; others are meant to live for hundreds of years. Some songs are meant to touch only one heart; others are meant to reach millions. Every song is worth the effort of creating it.

Outside of my relationship with God and with my family and friends, songwriting is probably the most precious gift in my life, and it is one of the most effective ways that I can connect with God. Time and again, God has spoken to me—He has had a message *just for me*—through my own songs.

One time, after I had written a song called "These Things Are True of You," a song about God's character, I was thinking about the truth that God never gives up on the hopeless ones. I thought, *Isn't God great! He never gives up on the drug addicts, the prostitutes, the homeless.* Later, when I was singing the song for my church for the first time, I heard God say, "No, Tommy, you're the hopeless one." I began to remember all the ways that I had failed and sinned, and I thought about how unworthy I was to serve God in the ways that I do—yet He lets me serve Him in such incredible ways. What a blessing it is when God speaks to you through your own song! It's His way of reminding you that the songs He gives you really are gifts from Him. They truly are "songs from heaven."

Sometimes God's message has a bigger audience. A few years ago, I was part of a worship evangelism crusade in the Philippines. Ten thousand people gathered in a soccer field to hear songs of worship.

When we gave the invitation, about 300 people came forward and prayed to receive Christ as their Lord and Savior. The first thing these new believers did when they were only minutes old in Christ was to worship God. As we all began to sing a tune I wrote called "How Could I but Love You," I wept as I heard thousands of voices passionately singing to their God. He made this possible through a song that started out as a simple, worshipful thought in my office one morning a few months before this event!

Stories have come to me of people singing one of my songs to loved ones as they took their last breath. It is almost incomprehensible to me that the last sound someone would hear on earth before entering eternity before the throne of God was a song of praise that He had given to me. When I received an e-mail describing how a suicidal teenager had chosen life when she heard one of my songs, I knew that although I was completely powerless to save her, God certainly wasn't. He used His power through just one song to reach that particular teenager's heart.

I am not relating stories about my songs to elevate myself. My hope is that you will be inspired by the potential impact that God places in *every* worship song and begin to write music for Him.

It is definitely a privilege and a joy to write worship songs, but it is also hard work. You may spend literally hours upon hours writing songs that will never reach the potential you had hoped for or that will fail to connect with a church congregation. You will experience disappointment and times of rejection in this process of writing. The good news is that God has millions of songs in His hand that He's just waiting to give us if we will remain faithful and make ourselves available to receive them.

I offer this little book to you with a sense of passion to see you, and others like you, experience the blessings of writing worship songs that God will use for His glory. Whether you write a song that reaches the nations or touches only a single heart, I pray that you will be inspired to write a song that will bring great honor and glory to our Lord and Savior Jesus Christ in a new, fresh and powerful way!

chapter 1

Worship Songs —Something Special

I believe that music was ultimately created to give glory to God, and that in God's eyes, worship songs are among the most precious, beautiful and valuable of art forms.

Worship songs are also special because they are the music of the people—the music of the average person. There is almost nothing more meaningful or fulfilling to me than knowing that I am helping someone express passionate worship to his or her Creator through my songs. For thousands of years the Lord has used the gift of music to touch people in a way that few other mediums of communication can.

You may have already realized that we're in the midst of a worship awakening. God is bestowing unusual favor on the gift of songwriting, and many of these songs are being written not only by seasoned professionals, but also by people who are simply worshipers expressing an inspirational thought or idea.

I believe that many people have been given this special gift and may not even be aware of it. I also believe that we have just begun to scratch the surface of the unique and various ways that worship songs can sound and how they will affect both those who are in the Church and those who are outside of the Church community. There will never be too many worship songs, for we will never be able to plumb the depth or span the breadth of how awesome God is and how much we owe Him! Worship songs are the songs that move God's heart.

CREATING WORSHIP SONGS

Whenever I have been asked to speak or teach at songwriting classes and workshops, I meet people who want to know how to be creative. Although I'm not at all sure that creativity can be taught, I hope that my words will inspire your creativity. I want to share with you the process I go through when I'm writing a worship song. I can tell you about some of the things that inspire me and some of the things that I listen for. I hope that you will take that information and tap into your own creativity to find a process—a creative style—that works for you. It will be something that is entirely unique to you.

Although there are books on songwriting that contain a by-the-book list of rules (some of which are quite helpful), many of these books encourage the songwriter to create by using an established formula. While rules for the art of songwriting are a great place to start and a fine way to learn, you shouldn't be afraid to break them. If you use *Songs from Heaven* in any way as you begin to explore the worship songs within you, please use what I say only as a set of guidelines—a jumping-off point for your own brand of creativity.

A NEW SONG FOR YOUR AUDIENCE OF ONE

The Bible verse at the beginning of this book is what I call my life verse. "He put a new song in my mouth, a hymn of praise to our God. Many will see and fear and will put their trust in the Lord" (Ps. 40:3). Here's my paraphrase: "Through letting people watch me or hear me live out my authentic, personal, spontaneous relationship with God, many of them will hunger for the same and put their trust in Him."

Singing a new song to the Lord is really nothing more then praying. During a worship concert, a woman shouted after the second song, "You forgot to pray!" and I responded, "Ma'am, that's what we've been doing." The good news is that everyone can pray, which means that everyone can sing a new song to the Lord. For some of you, the melody may be only two or three notes, but if that melody is sung from your heart, it is a beautiful sound to your heavenly father.

This book exists mostly to inspire songwriting, but my hope is that in its words you will find the challenge to keep your relationship with God fresh and creative. Our God is not just a higher power. He is a relational "God with us" kind of God, and He is blessed when His children say they love Him in new and heartfelt ways.

There have been many times, especially during my early songwriting years, when I would write and perform a song alone in my room for the sole purpose of blessing my audience of One. During those times, I would say, "God, this one is just for You!" Your greatest success, my brother or sister, will always be to touch the heart of God. I encourage you to not only say your prayers but to *sing* your prayers. This will bless your Father God, the author of all creativity, and deepen your relationship with Him. And just maybe He will take your little song to the world so that many will see and reverence Him and put their trust in Him!

chapter 2

How I Write Songs

The most honest and helpful method of teaching that I can offer to you is to literally describe the process I use when writing a worship song. So let's get started with a few examples of how songs come to me.

In the morning, usually following a time of devotions, I meditate on one specific thought that has come to me either through reading the Word or through prayer. Most creative people will tell you that they have a specific time of day (or night) when they are the most productive. I suggest that you try to identify when that time of day is for you and make it a point to reserve it just for songwriting. My most creative time happens to be in the morning. That's when I'll pick up my guitar and begin strumming in a musical style that best seems to communicate the thought I'm working with; I then just begin to worship. I search for a catch phrase, or hook, that best describes the thought. If I can find that one line, half the battle is over. Many times the phrase will already be found in the Scripture I've been reading.

At this point, I'm already thinking about how I can create music that will enable the average person to sing along and be touched by this one phrase or truth. In other words, I try to keep the melody within one octave and the rhythmical phrasing of the lyrics consistent and as simple as possible.

When the song starts to take form, it's time to ask myself a couple of important questions: Does the song sound too much like some other song? Is the song too predictable? Even if the answer to these questions is yes, it's not necessarily time to give up on pursuing the song.

If the song seems to have potential, I'll focus on changing the melody slightly by changing the rhythm or groove of the song, or both. None of us can escape the fact that frequently a new song will be inspired by some other song. There's nothing wrong with that. But when you're listening to your new song, consciously think about what parts of it sound exactly like the song it reminds you of and tweak those parts to make them sound different.

For me, this is where the real work usually begins. Although I have the basic idea of the music and the lyrical hook of the chorus, I must now come up with all the other lyrics that will complete the song. I find it helpful to look up Scripture references that go along with the original text or theme, and I also use my computer thesaurus to find just the right words. My goal in doing this is to avoid using the same phrases that I have used in a previous song. This approach always forces me to be creative when writing lyrics.

As I continue to get ideas, I sing and play them into a handheld digital recorder. I find that using a small portable recording device such as this is a good way to make sure that a fleeting but great idea doesn't get away. I'm always looking for interesting or new chord progressions that will serve as a fresh sound bed for the lyrics to rest on. I also listen for the correct tempo and the type of groove the drums will play.

When all the basics of the song are in place—when the framework is complete—it's time to listen analytically to the song. Often when I play back a song, I will get new ideas. Of course there are times when I find myself beginning to dislike what I've put together and wonder why I wasted my time, but when that happens, I take a break and come back to the song at a later time. A little time and distance can work wonders for objectivity.

Once I return to a song, if it's pretty much complete and seems to have even a little potential, I play it for a few people whom I can count on for honest feedback. In my case, two of those people include my wife and my pastor. It is extremely important that every songwriter have an honest, straightforward and objective friend who can serve as a sounding board for new songs and new song ideas. Ideally it will be someone you can trust—someone who loves you and wants you to succeed. Of course, it's also a huge plus if your sounding board has a proven ear for a good song. If you are blessed with more than one objective listener, that's even better.

If my new song passes the listening test of my wife and pastor, I then teach it to the congregation of my church. Most of the time, I know right away if the song is "the bomb" or just "a bomb." I also generally try to keep the song in our worship services for two or three weeks in a row. Giving up on a new song too soon might eliminate the opportunity to see if it is gradually being accepted and embraced by the congregation.

In a nutshell, that's how I approach writing a worship song. Now let's look at the components of songwriting in more detail.

chapter 3

Inspiration —Where Worship Songs Come From

When was the last time you were completely undone by the wonder that is God and by all that He has created? We are in awe of the vastness of His galaxies and what lies beyond the stars and the beauty we see in the night sky. When we wonder about these things, we are using imagination— which is also created by God. And what an incredible gift to us! Yet we don't use this gift often enough in positive and productive ways. Let's expand that thought a bit.

The universe, at one time, existed only in God's imagination. Every object made by man at one time existed only in someone's imagination. Therefore, when you write a worship song, you imagine it in your mind before you ever touch a guitar or keyboard and before you sing even a single word of the lyrics.

If you find yourself stumped and can't think of how to write your song, it's time to go deep into your imagination and connect with what you feel God is saying to you. Analyze your life and what God is speaking into your current situation. Philippians 4:8 encourages us to think of "whatever is true, whatever is noble, whatever is right, whatever is pure, whatever is lovely, whatever is admirable—if anything is excellent or praiseworthy—think about such things." Fill your mind with the good things of God, and dare to dream! Nothing will be more powerful in helping you write your songs than a Spirit-led imagination.

I find it crucial to my songwriting process to stay tuned in to my imagination. For instance, I challenge myself to imagine a song that will make a hard-hearted person cry or a person burdened with sadness laugh. I try to imagine a song played at a fast tempo but with slow, drawn-out lyrical phrases

or a shuffle in a minor key, or maybe the entire congregation shouting out a rap. I love to dream about
these things, and I constantly play out different
song scenarios in my mind.

Inspiration from Events

I'll never forget that dreadful morning of September
11, 2001. I was in Pennsylvania with my friend Bob
Wilson, the drummer on our worship team. A ring-
ing phone woke me up. We were told to turn on the
TV. We watched the television screen in horror as the
towers fell, and I began to weep at the thought of
how many people were losing their lives. Suddenly
the hymn "The Solid Rock" started to run through
my head ("On Christ the solid Rock, I stand; all
other ground is sinking sand . . ."). I thought, *When
tragedy strikes and our world crumbles around us, we
always and forever will have our solid rock and cornerstone,
Jesus, to stand on. There will never be a devilish act strong
enough to separate us from God's love or knock us off that
firm foundation.*

I have always deeply loved that hymn "The Solid
Rock," but as I had done many times before, I wanted
to express the truth found in its words in a new way.
My song "There Is a Rock" began to come together in

my mind as a response to that violent day in the history of our country.

> *The nations are searching for something that's*
>   *absolutely true*
> *So now we declare it, Jesus, all truth is found in*
>   *You.*
>
> *There is a Rock, a solid Rock*
> *A Rock we've built our lives upon.*
> *There is a hope, a blessed hope*
> *So we now shout it to the world.* [1]

Many times, a declarative type of song is fast and loud so that it communicates joy and celebration, but I was picturing in my mind music and lyrics that were passionate and declarative. I wanted the groove on the chorus to boldly reinforce the blessed hope of our Christian faith. The lyrics and music of "There Is a Rock" developed in such a way as to declare the absolute truth of our unshakable God.

Inspiration from Devotions or Quiet Times

The lyrics to the song "What a Good God You've Been to Me" came as a simple and honest response to a personal devotional time I had with the Lord. I was looking back on my life and thinking about my wife and kids, and my calling as a worship leader. I became fixed on the goodness of my God. This song was quite personal, and I thought that I would only sing it one time as an offertory at my church. I then forgot about it until some time later, when a friend who had been bedridden and fighting a serious illness came up to me and asked when I would sing "What a Good God You Are to Me" again. I could hardly remember the song, but someone had recorded the service when I sang the song and had given the tape to this woman. She had listened to it over and over again while on her sick bed. When I listened to the tape, it brought the song back to my memory. I still sing it today when I travel, because it so honestly expresses my heartfelt gratitude to God.

> *What a good God You've been to me*
> *Your goodness and Your grace every day I've seen*
> *What else can I do but give thanks to You*
> *What a good God You've been to me.*[2]

Luke 6:46 states, "Out of the abundance of the heart the mouth speaks." As you fill your heart and mind with God's Word, His words will automatically flow out of you and into your songs. About 80 percent of my songs come out of personal times of devotion with the Lord. In fact, the songwriting process has evolved into a main part of my time with God.

A regular and consistent quiet time with God is also a great way to handle the busyness and stresses of contemporary life. I have never written a song when I was dealing with the kind of pressure that comes from trying to do too much. (How can God inspire us with a new song if our minds are too cluttered, too noisy or too busy to hear Him?) Seek time alone with God to get things back in perspective and to become more receptive to His ways and His thoughts, which includes receptivity to song ideas.

Inspiration from the Good Times and the Bad Times

The song "Lord, I Run to You" was definitely inspired by a bad time. I had hurt my back and was in pain for nearly a year. Although I had been to the doctor, done exercises, tried doctor-prescribed painkillers and, of course, had people praying for me, the pain continued. I was in my office one morning, feeling mad and discouraged. I thought, *I've tried everything, and once again there is nowhere else to run but to Him. He's the one who made me, and He will sustain me. Every other option is utterly futile.* So I looked up every verse I could think of that would inspire me to run to Him. I said, *God, give me words and a melody that will inspire my faith to turn to You and to no one and nothing else.*

As usual, God the Redeemer turned my bad time into a song that has helped many people cry out to God in ways their hearts were longing to do.

Lord, I run to You, no one else will do
Though my heart and flesh may fail,
You're my everpresent help,
My tower of strength, my portion evermore.[3]

The chords at the end of the verses to this song, beginning with the lyrics "Though my heart and flesh may fail," were inspired by chromatically walking down with the roots. In the key of A, I started on an F, which is a half-step up from the Five chord, and played the roots, only I played F, E, E♭, (I couldn't make D work, so I skipped it) D♭, C, B, then back to F and the Five chord E7. This is one of those songs that keyboard players love, but guitar players hate!

Writing a worship song can bring a release to your spirit like few things can. When I'm in the midst of extreme circumstances, whether good or bad, I make a conscious effort to evaluate the details of the situation and decide if the circumstances—good, bad or both—should be communicated in a song.

I remember calling Andy, my best friend from childhood, shortly after finding out that he had an inoperable brain tumor. I wanted to comfort Andy and ease his burden. My thoughts eventually focused on the truth that no matter how horrible the circumstances and no matter how difficult things may seem, God is always with us.

I turned to one of my favorite psalms and read, "God is our refuge and strength, an ever present help in trouble. Therefore we will not fear, though the earth give way and the mountains fall into the heart of the sea" (Ps. 46:1-2). This was the message I needed to communicate to my friend in song. Out of that Scripture came the song "Be Still and Know." The hook line is:

> *Therefore we have hope and we will not fear*
> *For our God is near.*[4]

"Be Still and Know" was eventually recorded at Christian Assembly Church, where I serve as worship leader, during our *Live At Home* concert. Whenever I hear this song, I think of Andy and all the other people who go through impossibly tough circumstances. Whether in this life or the life to come, there is always hope, for our God is near.

Inspiration from Sermons and Worship Services

Now and then you can look to your very own pastor for inspiration for a great song idea. Whenever I'm in a church service or at a conference, I always keep my ears open for the moment the lyrical hook, or theme, shows up (see chapter 6 for more about the hook).

Special teaching seminars and church Bible studies can also lead you to your next worship song. The very nature of a Bible study focuses on the details of God's Word, which can act as a flashing neon sign for the theme of your next song.

Many times, I get song ideas in the midst of a worship set or at the end of the set when my pastor is closing our time of music. You, too, can get some of your best ideas during such a time. Your biggest challenge with this particular moment of inspiration will be to remember the idea, because you have to wait until the end of the service before you can get your idea down on tape!

The song "How Good and Pleasant" is an example of such an inspirational moment for me. This song came spontaneously at the end of a service late one Sunday night at a church I was visiting in Canada. There was an amazing sense of unity and joy shared by everyone in the room. The next thing I knew, I was singing:

> *How good and pleasant it is when we dwell*
> *together in unity*
> *And Praise the Lord, Praise the Lord*
> *Praise the Lord, Praise the Lord*
> *Praise the Lord, Praise the Lord.*[5]

I added the bridge ("Showers of blessings . . .") later, but most of the song originated during that church service.

Inspiration from Listening to Music

How many times have you heard a great song and thought, *Wow, I sure would like to write a song like that someday!* That's why listening to music should be an important part of your songwriting life.

I make myself listen to all kinds of music—even musical styles that I don't necessarily prefer. I've made an effort to embrace a wide spectrum of musical ideas, and I'm still learning how to hear what makes a great song, regardless of what genre it comes from. The Latin groove on the song "Mourning into Dancing" actually emerged from hearing a car commercial on television!

The turnarounds keyboard players use in black gospel music (a turnaround is a series of chords usually found at the end of a section in a song to get back to the main chord) can provide another opportunity for inspiration. By the way, learning chord progressions and turnarounds from your favorite songs can be a great way to broaden your musical palate. Howard McCrary is a musician who has greatly inspired me. He's one of the only people I've seen who seems to sit and watch while God plays through his fingers. I recorded him playing with us at a concert, and for weeks I studied some of the turnarounds he would spontaneously pull off.

I learned one turnaround from him in particular that I was able to tweak in such a way as to make it repeatable. The chords are

Bm7[b5], E7, Am7, D7, Gm7, C7, F

Originally it ended there, but then from the F, I added F, Gm7, G#dim, F7/A so that the phrase could be repeated. For two weeks, I played this phrase every time I picked up my guitar. One day, when I read Psalm 66, I thought, *That's it! These lyrics and those chords go together!* Psalm 66 speaks of making God's praise glorious and excellent, and that's what (at least to me) this turnaround communicates. "Make It Glorious" was written from only one verse and one turnaround. Everything else in the song was filled in later.

When I realized that these lyrics and chords would go together, I had just taken my family out to dinner. As we were walking across the parking lot to our car, I saw the whole picture in my head. Interestingly enough, creativity often comes when you're in the midst of doing something ordinary. You know it's true! How many times have you had your greatest brainstorm while you were in the shower?

Inspiration from a Change of Scenery

Sometimes the song ideas just pour out and it seems like they'll never stop coming. Other times you wonder if you'll ever have another original thought. Our minds can get stuck in a rut when we try to work out a single problem or try to sort out too many problems at once.

Everybody needs to recharge their batteries now and then. For me, going for a walk or a drive alone can clear my mind and help me focus. Getting out of the office, breathing some fresh air and giving my eyes something to look at besides the same four walls restores me. What kinds of things recharge your battery?

Inspiration from Above

Two of my favorite secular songs are "Somewhere Over the Rainbow" from *The Wizard of Oz* and "Somewhere (A Place For Us)" from *West Side Story*. They both have masterfully written melodies and make me think of heaven. Heaven is a theme in several of my songs because it is my ultimate source of wonder and hope. You can't have worship without wonder. To wonder, ponder and hunger for the limitless attributes of our future eternal home is a healthy part of our Christian walk. Heaven is also the only place of hope and comfort when we're grieving the loss of a loved one or the loss of a lifelong dream.

Not long ago I was told that a Christian man who was on his deathbed and had his family around him was catapulted into eternity while listening to and singing "Never Gonna Stop." Wow! What greater reward could you have as a songwriter?

I wrote "Never Gonna Stop" when I visited my parents' mobile home during the time they lived in Desert Hot Springs, California. I had just spent a lovely evening hanging out and singing hymns with them and was getting ready for bed. I felt so grateful for my Christian heritage. Suddenly the thought came that although my parents were getting up in years, what we had just done that evening was something I would do with them, and the rest of my Christian family, forever.

Nothing can communicate eternal truths like music can! When you write songs about heaven, you can hear the timeless qualities that God put inside the various notes and rhythms. Music truly is a gift from our infinite and eternal God.

chapter 4

Creating the Music

If you are just beginning to write songs, you might want to start with a process I call "modeling." What I mean by modeling is spending time listening to what other songwriters have written—the songs that work and the songs that touch you. When you find a simple song that you really like, use some of the same elements to write your own version. I'm not suggesting that you plagiarize someone else's material. I'm saying that as a method of developing your songwriting skills, you can model your song on that of an established writer.

Getting Started
As you're learning to become a better songwriter, use modeling to create all components of your song.

If you play an instrument, figure out the chords of the other song. If there's an interesting chord progression in either the verse or chorus, concentrate on those elements. While you're working on your lyrics, experiment by using the same number of syllables in each line of the phrases from the song you're using as a model. Although you wouldn't present the song that you come up with as your own, this is a great way to learn the songwriting craft. You can also write songs over the rhythm patterns of other recordings to help you acquire a feel for a variety of rhythms.

Once you begin to develop a sense of how songs are constructed, you can take the process a little further. Start to alter the chords of the song that you're modeling, and then try singing a different melody along with the new chords. Next, find a favorite psalm or poem and choose a couple of verses that work for you. The song might not be a great one, or it may still sound too much like the original song, but that's all right at this stage—you're simply trying to get started. I think you'll be surprised at how well you do if you don't put pressure on yourself to write something awesome the first few times out of the gate.

Matching Melodies and Words

When you're analyzing what you have written, always ask yourself if your music relays the same message as your lyrics.

The song "Mourning Into Dancing" was born when I heard the text of Psalm 30 sung to a rather sad melody. For me, the tone of the music—the feeling it projected—didn't seem to match the message of the words of the psalm. I thought the text called for bright and cheerful music that would make people want to dance.

I knew that I would someday compose music that would be a better match for this passage. Years later, I saw a car commercial that inspired the music I wrote to accompany my version of the psalm.

Forward, Always Forward

Once you begin working on a new worship song, it's important to keep your momentum and not get bogged down in the details. If you're making great progress with a melody but a section of lyrics is giving you trouble, you might feel tempted to stop there and try to fix it. If you do that, you may lose your forward momentum. In order not to get bogged down, a helpful technique that many songwriters use is to sing melodies with lyrics that make no sense.

From the earliest days of my songwriting, I mumbled nonsense syllables and words to help me find the melodies for my songs. This seems to be a common practice. For instance, "Yesterday," by Paul McCartney and John Lennon, is one of the most covered songs in pop music history. Sir Paul has made it known in many interviews throughout the years that the title and main lyric of this monster hit was originally "Scrambled Eggs," and that it remained "Scrambled Eggs" for several days while he developed the song.

The main idea is to avoid letting a little snag in the creative process stop you in your tracks. If you have a good idea for a melody, then move forward with it. If you think that you must have the perfect lyric before you can proceed, you run the risk of not finishing your song at all.

Song Dynamics

Songs are more interesting and engaging if they actually take you on a musical journey. I like songs that build from soft melodies in lower registers to loud, high climaxes, as in "How Could I But Love You" and "Be Still and Know." These songs begin softly, build to a climax and then return to softness, leaving you with a feeling of peace.

As a basic rule of thumb, verses tend to be written in lower registers and gradually climb to the higher register where the chorus takes over. Generally, a well-structured song will steadily build and climax at the end of the chorus. I also try to save the more significant and meaningful words, such as "Lord," "love" and "You," for the end of an ascending phrase.

The Melody Test

The key to making your song more likely to pass the test of having a memorable melody is simplicity. It's easy to overdo it. We have so many ideas, so many feelings, and a life so full of complexities. Resist the urge to pack too much into one song.

The chorus of "Amen" is an example of simplicity. The entire text consists of the word "amen," and the melody, for the most part, is sung in a two-note grouping. The first "amen" moves from an A note to a G#. The second time the word is sung, it moves from an F# back up to a G#. Then the A to G# is repeated. The chorus resolves with a six-note figure, again sung on the word "amen."

"He Knows My Name" is another example of simplicity. The lyric in the verse expresses a simple idea—

that God created us and He knows us intimately:

> *I have a Maker,*
> *He formed my heart.*
> *Before even time began my life was in His hand.*

Musically, the melody line of the verse stays within a six-note range. In the key of E, the melody actually uses only five notes between middle C and the A above middle C. The chorus emphasizes the main theme of the song:

> *He knows my name.*
> *He knows my every thought.*
> *He sees each tear that falls,*
> *And hears me when I call.*[6]

The lyric in the chorus doesn't wander from the theme, and the melody also stays within a six-note range. The lines are short and each touches on a variation of what the song is about. Only five notes are used between E (above middle C) and C (an octave above middle C).

When I wrote "He Knows My Name," I didn't make a conscious decision to use a specific number of notes in the melody line. But the small number of notes creates a built-in limitation to how complex the melody can become. Keeping the melody of your song simple makes it possible to communicate your main idea more easily, and it makes the song more memorable. Although writing simply is one of the hardest things to achieve, it's well worth the effort.

Most Western music written less then a century ago depended (musically speaking) entirely on the melody. In modern music, the rhythms and the grooves allow us to get away with melodies that really have little to them. This is especially true in worship music because, as I've already said, simple is usually better. The problem is that worship CDs are beginning to sound the same. When I wrote "Jesus, We Celebrate Your Fame," I tried to find a melody that could truly stand on its own. I began to play and sing intervals that I didn't commonly use, such as 1-5, 2-5, 3-1 (these numbers represent the notes in a 7-note major scale, regardless the key). Although this pattern didn't provide the greatest melody in the world, the verses of the song can be sung a cappella and still make sense.

Another interesting fact about this song is that it is in 5/4 time. When I came up with the melody and began adding chords, I realized that the melody didn't fit into 4/4 time. However, this time I decided not to let the groove win out and I let the melody dictate the time signature.

By the way, you might consider using this song to audition your church drummers; it's not often that they have to worship God while counting to 5!

Make It Different

A songwriter may be in love with the last song he or she wrote, or the song before that, and those songs may be perfect in every way. But let's face it, we don't want all of our songs to sound alike.

If I discover that my latest melody sounds like another song, whether it's one of mine or someone else's, I alter the part of the tune that sounds the most familiar. (Make sure the original melody has been well altered!) When I do this, I generally find that at first I don't like the altered melody. My ears have become so accustomed to the original tune that the new melody sounds like a mistake. As I keep repeating the new line, it quickly begins to sound as if it was always meant to be that way.

Try Something New

One of the things I love about the song "No Greater

Love" is that even though it has a fun, celebrative groove, it seems to inspire heartfelt worship. Years ago, there was a notion that fast songs were praise songs and slow songs were worship songs. Although many times this is true, it's certainly not a rule. The joy of creativity allows you to break the rules and the boundaries of the past and see what great new things can happen! I've had the privilege of watching people sing "No Greater Love" with dancing in their feet and tears of joy in their eyes— that deep joy that comes only in the midst of God's manifest presence. What a blessing to see God touch people in such a deep way through something as simple and seemingly shallow as a hip-hop worship song!

Sometimes I try a different form, structure or style simply for the sake of creativity. The rebel in me always wants to prove the by-the-book songwriting rules wrong. Some of our best worship songs have come about because somebody broke all the rules and created something awesome.

I believe that the greatest reason to be innovative is that it reflects the very nature of God. He is the ultimate creator and innovator and must surely enjoy it when His children mirror Him in this way.

chapter 5

Writing Lyrics

Writing lyrics can be a songwriter's greatest challenge. Most of us need all the help we can get!

One type of worship song that is easier to write than most—and one that is the most effective—is the worship song written directly from Scripture. I would say that approximately half of my songs fall into this category. I highly recommend this approach, because it's hard to go wrong when using the Word of God. Using Scripture as inspiration can be especially helpful to those who struggle with the lyrical side of songwriting.

The Scripture you draw into your song does not have to be word for word. But if you're not going to use a verse word for word, make sure you're absolutely certain that you understand what the passage is saying so that you can communicate God's truth in the way He originally intended. When I use Scripture for my lyrics, usually I read the verse in several different

Bible translations. Bible commentaries on the verse can also provide helpful inspiration. Frequently this process gives me new ideas. Once I'm confident that I fully comprehend the Scripture text, I feel total freedom to be creative with it.

The song "Everyone Arise" serves as a good example of using Scripture in lyrics. This song is based on Isaiah 60:1-2, which reads in the *New International Version,* "Arise, shine for your light has come, and the glory of the LORD rises upon you. See, darkness covers the earth and thick darkness is over the peoples, but the LORD rises upon you." I also used a portion of Psalm 34 in the song, which states, "Those who look to Him are radiant" (v. 5). I love these passages because they communicate the vision of worship evangelism. They tell us that the world will see God's glory through us as we look to the Lord and give our lives in worship to Him.

Here's how these verses of Scripture were used in "Everyone Arise":

> *Everyone arise and let it shine,*
> *Children of our God your light has come,*
> *For the glory of the Lord*

And the beauty of His grace
Is rising on you now.

The song's chorus is simply a response to the text:

Praise Him, praise Him, praise Him.
Arise and shine and celebrate Him.
Let His glory rise on you, let it rise.[7]

The presence of Scripture is strong in this song, and I was able to harness the power of God's Word without quoting Scripture word for word.

For centuries, Christians have recited God's Word together, and there is a supernatural power that comes from it. Reciting Scripture in song is a tradition we need to keep alive. So give it a try in your songs!

Rhyme

One of the elements that make lyrics such a challenge to the songwriter is the necessity for rhyme. Because our ears are so accustomed to hearing rhyme in songs, there is really no way around it. The only time I don't worry too much about rhyme, at least true rhyme, is when I'm writing a worship song that draws heavily from Scripture. This is especially true when I'm taking a more word-for-word approach.

Contemporary lyrics tend to more closely imitate the sound of everyday conversation than lyrics from 40 or 50 years ago, which is an important reason to write honestly and avoid rhyming just for the sake of rhyming. Every rhyme should sound natural and be motivated by the message in the song's phrase. The best rhymes are those that rhyme perfectly but still have the natural sound of human speech.

Rhyming lyrics make phrases sound smooth and beautiful. They also make lyrics memorable. Words that rhyme tend to act as a key for recalling the rest of the phrases.

Coming up with rhyming lyrics can be a very time consuming task. I find that it's like putting together a puzzle (not my favorite pastime); but the process is necessary and frequently rewarding when all the pieces snap into place. I try to avoid letting rhymes determine what I'm trying to say. Yet there have been instances when the search for a rhyme led me to writing a lyric that was more profound than what I originally had in mind.

There are two styles of rhyme: true rhyme and false rhyme. Here are a few examples of true rhyme:

Hand—Land
Hurt—Dessert
Make—Shake
Descend—Amend

The chorus of "That's Why We Praise Him" employs a true rhyme.

That's why we praise Him, that's why we sing.
That's why we offer Him our everything.[8]

Another song verse that incorporates true rhyme is found in "Let's Think About Our God."

Let's think about our God, our Savior and our King.
The One who gave it all, He gave up everything.
Let's think about the Man who shed His precious
   blood,
So we could be His friend, His friends until the end.[9]

The end of the first and second lines derive their rhyme on the "ing" of "King" and "everything." The fourth line utilizes an internal rhyme with the two rhyming words located within the same line—in this case they are "friend" and "end."

A few examples of false rhyme include:

Sighed—Cry
Hands—Man
Mind—Time
Lie—Fight

You can see that false rhyme relies on the strength of the vowel sounds to link two words together, while the consonants take something of a back seat.

The verse of "Only a God Like You" is a good example of false rhyme.

For the praises of man
I will never, ever stand
For the kingdoms of this world
I'll never give my heart away or shout my praise.[10]

The first line ends with the word "man," and the word "stand" completes the false rhyme at the end of the second line. Since "man" ends with the letter "n" and "stand" ends in "nd," the rhyme is dependent on the sound of the vowel "a," which is common to both words.

You might want to note that contemporary music often mixes true and false rhymes within the same song—which is fine as long as it sounds right and natural. The chorus of "Lord I Believe in You" uses a combination of true and false rhyme.

> *Lord I believe in You. I'll always believe in You*
> *Though I can't see You with my eyes*
> *Deep in my heart Your presence I find*
> *Lord I believe in You and I'll keep my trust in You*
> *Let the whole world say what they may*
> *No one can take this joy away.*
> *Lord I believe.*[11]

The second and third lines false rhyme the "i" sound of "eyes" and "find." The fifth and sixth lines use a true rhyme with "may" and "away."

Here are a few more suggestions for using rhyme:

- Don't hesitate to use a good rhyming dictionary to help you find the right rhyme. I have a software version installed on my computer.
- If you're just starting out, you might want to begin by using true rhymes before you move on to the using false rhymes.
- Be consistent and use the same rhyme scheme from verse to verse whenever you can. This

will give cohesiveness to your song.

- Try testing your lyrics as though you're an actor reading dialogue. When you read your lyrics, do they "talk"? Do they sound like normal, human speech?

Let It Flow

As I discussed earlier in regard to melody, it is important that you keep your ideas flowing. This applies to lyrics, as well. When ideas for lyrics begin to come, don't over analyze them. Avoid the risk of interrupting the creative flow by putting *all* of your ideas on paper, or record them. Even making notes of the ideas that are not so good gives you more to work with.

Don't Say Too Much

When I read the Bible, I often get excited by its many truths. But I have learned that the inherent beauty of a worship song lies in its ability to communicate something simple in a very deep and meaningful way. If I have several different thoughts, I put each thought into a different song. Your goal as a songwriter is to help people who hear your worship song grasp the one central theme and focus on that truth.

"Here I Am Again" is definitely a song that doesn't say too much! In fact, I sometimes laugh when I sing this song because it came to me when I was trying to write a lyrically profound song. As I sat and stared at my paper, with no words coming to mind, I started to think about how many worship songs, mine included, seem to say the same thing. That number-one theme would have to be telling God "I love You." So in a sense, "Here I Am Again" is about how I couldn't think of anything else to say but, "Oh, how I love You!" In truth, I believe that we will never be able to say these words enough to our God. This song sounds celebrative, but to me it came out sounding worshipful. (At least that's what happens when we sing it at my church.)

Write from the Heart

As writers, it is our job to help other people express authentic worship to God. The more truthful the feeling and emotion we place in a song, the less contrived and insincere it will sound. To do that, we have to have experienced authentic worship ourselves.

I find that I have to search deep in my heart and spend extended times of quiet before the Lord in order to reach a place of real honesty. The song

"Lord, I Believe in You" was written during a time of great struggle in my faith. Disappointments and unanswered prayers had filled me with doubt and discouragement. Yet deep in my heart, I knew that I believed. I began to realize that I needed a way to declare the truth to myself as well as to everyone around me. Even though I couldn't see God with my eyes, I could find His spirit deep in my heart. I declared that message in the song "Lord, I Believe in You." What a release of faith this song was for me and has been for others.

But Will It Make a Good Song?

There are many truths in God's Word and many words that He speaks to our hearts. But not all of them are meant to be a song.

People often encourage me to write a song to a passage of Scripture that has inspired them in a personal way. But there are many wonderful truths in God's Word that are simply not musical. Here are a few examples that don't work for me.

- Managing money in a godly way (my pastor often speaks about this, but it's not really song material).

- Raising children in a godly way and with Christ-like goals (a great truth, but I wouldn't necessarily write a song about it).
- Something controversial like speaking in tongues (you may be very passionate about the subject in one way or another, but I think you're better off talking about it as opposed to singing about it).

Some of the themes that have worked well for me that I frequently see in worship songs include:

- Direct praise and worship ("Unto The King," "Holy")
- Surrender ("These Things Are True of You")
- Mission ("Why Did He Save You," "As We Worship You")
- Love and devotion ("When All Is Said and Done," "How Could I But Love You")
- Declaration ("That's Why We Praise Him," "Lift Up Your Heads")
- Faith and trust ("Lord, I Believe in You," "Joy, Joy, Joy")
- God's love, mercy and grace ("No Greater Love," "His Love Endures Forever")

- Heaven ("It Will Be Worth It All," "When We See Him")
- God's presence ("Sweet Presence of Jesus," "Where You Are")
- Repentance ("Calling Out to You")
- The name of Jesus ("Jesus That Name," "Jesus Your Name")

You can get even more ideas of what type of themes make good worship songs by going to the nearest Christian music store and looking at the track list of any CD. In most cases the really good song ideas are the ones that end up getting recorded. Great songwriters have developed an ear and an eye for the concepts and ideas that will work as a song. My experience has been that if I can find a great theme, the songwriting process will require half the work but produce twice the result!

The song "Calling Out to You" is a prayer of repentance taken from 2 Chronicles 7:14. I knew of an older song called "If My People," the lyrics of which followed that Scripture passage word for word; but I thought that for my church community a new expression would be helpful. The interesting twist to the story behind "Calling Out to You" is that I wrote it just before 9/11 and was in the middle of recording it. When I arrived home after a conference in Pennsylvania, during which time 9/11 occurred, I immediately completed the recording and made it available as a free download for a period of time. I heard many reports of churches using it to renew their commitment to Christ in the midst of that tragic time.

Song Pictures and Emotions

Two things that I look for when writing lyrics are words that create pictures and stir the emotions. Let's take a look once again at "Mourning Into Dancing." Those three words in the title are all about emotions. They encourage us to picture people weeping and having a life-changing experience that turns into ecstatic joy.

Another good example of picture words can be found in the song "How Good and Pleasant." This song comes from Psalm 133: "For the Lord bestows His blessing, even life forevermore" (v. 3). Instead of duplicating that verse, in the bridge of the song I wrote:

Showers of blessing, showers they fall.
When we love and live in unity,
When we lift one voice loud and strong.[12]

"Showers of blessing" is a phrase that uses picture words. You can visualize God's blessings descending on the congregation as they sing in unity. It's a very simple phrase, yet it catches people's imagination and draws them into the song.

Passion, Creativity and Accessibility

If someone asked me what were the three most important ingredients of a good worship song, I would tell them passion, creativity and accessibility.

I want my songs to communicate the sincere, authentic passion for God that I feel in my heart. I want my songs to stir up that same kind of passion in the hearts of the people who hear and sing them. God wants us all to be on fire for Him. My prayer is that my songs will kindle that kind of fire in many hearts.

I also want my songs to touch people in fresh, creative ways. People are much more likely to keep listening when they hear a song that is a little different than other songs. Also, different people are touched in a variety of different ways. The creative approach of one song might draw a particular person closer to God even as its message is totally lost on another. I believe that the more I find creative approaches for worship songs, the more people my songs will have the potential of reaching.

Finally, I want my worship songs to be accessible. I want the average person to easily sing them. If you write a wonderful song, but only a trained and accomplished vocalist can sing it, the song's effectiveness will be limited.

If your song contains these three qualities of passion, creativity and accessibility, and if you're communicating God's truth in a clear and simple way, you will truly have a song that is something special.

chapter 6

Song Form and Structure

Contemporary song form began to evolve early in the twentieth century. By the early 1920s, songwriters generally composed popular songs containing two sections—a short introductory section called the verse, which established the topic described in the lyrics, and the chorus (or refrain). The title of the song was most often found within the chorus.

When experienced music industry professionals realized that they could increase record and sheet music sales by emphasizing the chorus, it became a common practice for performers to sing a song's chorus several times, which served to anchor the song title in the listener's memory.

Contemporary popular songs usually are longer and contain more words than songs written 50 to 60 years ago. Although the separate introductory section is no longer found in popular songs, the verse-chorus form has remained the most popular song structure. Today's songs generally consist of two or three verses that alternate with the chorus. Most contemporary choruses still contain the title of the song, as well as the main theme.

Contemporary worship songs have adopted this basic verse-chorus structure. The verse sets up or explains the theme of the chorus, and the chorus carries the theme. The chorus may also serve to anchor the theme in the listener's memory through repetition. This is readily apparent in both contemporary worship music and the beautiful old hymns of the past.

OLD GEMS IN NEW SETTINGS

I have written mostly about how to find and express the worship songs that God has given to you. I also want to talk briefly about the songs of others. If you want to bless the heart of the Father, consider arranging someone else's song to inspire young and old to worship together. I've seen this happen when I've arranged hymns, and it certainly is a taste of heaven. After all, fathers like it when their kids are all having fun together!

I enjoy arranging hymns and adding a bridge or chorus to them. Hymns, however, can present challenges when you attempt to make them work for all worshipers. The first challenge is to find the right tempo. Hymns, many times, are sung at such a fast tempo that it is hard to take in the richness of the lyrics. The second challenge is to find the kind of chorus that explains and sums up the lyrics in the verses and delivers the musical climax of the message. The third challenge is to find a new presentation—although hymns have served the Church in utterly profound ways for centuries, there is a need to present their power in a fresh way. (What I'm calling the third challenge is actually something that should energize any budding songwriter!)

Hymns are usually statements and declarations of our Christian theology. What hymns lack musically when compared with more modern praise songs they provide in voicing the life-changing truths of our faith. This is one reason why we will always need a healthy diet of psalms, hymns and spiritual songs (see Col. 3:16).

One more thought about hymns: Their lyrics tie us to our heritage as believers. We are part of a long line of courageous, creative and devoted people who were Christ-followers. When we sing their hymns, in a sense we join those who have gone before us. The more years you have lived, the more you will appreciate what a treasure it is to be a part of such a wonderful family!

Arranging a hymn is surprisingly easy to do. Usually, all that is required is a melody that rides a little bit above the verses and lyrics, the words of which are taken from the title and theme of the hymn. A simple example of a hymn I arranged was Philip B. Bliss's hymn "Hallelujah, What a Savior!" The first stanza reads,

> *"Man of Sorrows," what a name! For the Son of*
>   *God, who came*
> *Ruined sinners to reclaim! Hallelujah, what a*
>   *Savior!*[13]

I slowed the tempo of the hymn and added a chorus with a melody that soulfully and reflectively repeats the words "Hallelujah, hallelujah, hallelujah—what a Savior!" This addition gives the worshiper time to soak in the doctrinal truths of the verses.

If you decide to arrange the work of another person, do so with a sense of fear and trembling. You are

adding to a masterpiece that God has chosen to pre-
serve and use to promote worship of His name—
sometimes throughout many centuries.

BASIC SONG STRUCTURE

Before I describe the basic components of a song,
here is a summary, with a few examples from songs I
have written, of forms or structures that are commonly used in all worship songs.

- *Verse-Chorus.* This is the most common and
  simple form for any kind of popular song.
  "He Knows My Name" is written in this form.
- *Verse-Chorus-Bridge.* Adding a bridge creates a
  worship song that can stand alone. Because
  the additional section provides contrast—
  something fresh or different—it makes it
  possible for a worship leader to arrange the
  song to last as long as needed. A bridge can
  also keep the song moving. This has become
  a favorite form of mine. In "That's Why We
  Praise Him," the "Hallelujah" section serves
  as the bridge. This song can be easily direct-
  ed in and out of the three sections, to create

      spontaneity, which is something I love.

- *Verse-Bridge.* In this form, the lyrical and musical hook or punch line is usually placed at the end of the verse instead of in the chorus. Songs using this structure tend to be shorter. This form is great for creating medleys, which are useful in creating a flow in worship. In Verse-Bridge songs you can also choose to sing only the verse, if this feels right at the time. "Jesus, That Name" utilizes the verse-bridge form.

There are other combinations, and there are many fine books on writing popular songs that cover the various forms in depth. But these are the basic forms that will work well for you as you create songs.

THE ELEMENTS OF A SONG

The Hook

The hook is a phrase in a song that communicates the song's theme. The hook might consist of both the song title (or some other memorable phrase) accompanied by a catchy melodic line. A good hook will create a unique picture in the listener's mind and remain long after the song is over.

To become memorable, hooks often use repetition of both lyrical and musical phrases. Good hooks, however, should not use repetition for repetition's sake. Also, a good hook will generally supply enough information to exist apart from the other sections of the song.

The hook is most often found in the chorus of the song, though hooks can also be effectively used in verses. If a hook appears in a verse, more often than not it will be found in the last line of each verse. Two of my songs that have clearly defined hooks are "These Things Are True of You" and "When All Is Said and Done."

As important as hooks are, if there were ever a type of song that could get away with not using a hook, it would be the worship song. It is fascinating to me that somehow our spirits never grow tired of repeating the same praise and worship phrases that we hear in so many songs—"I worship You," "with all of my heart," "I sing praises," "I love You, Lord," "I bow down," to name a few.

Something deep within us cries out to sing these words to God, and obviously there is nothing wrong

with that. However, I try to look for a unique phrase
on which to hang the entire song—a phrase that will
give a song its own unique identity. Songs that contain standard worship phrases are great, but a song
that contains a strong hook to hang those same
phrases on is even better.

The Bridge

In addition to the verse and chorus, the bridge (or
release) is an optional third section that can be used
in contemporary songwriting structure. Musically,
the bridge should provide contrast to the verse and
chorus. Lyrically, it should make a new statement or
at least provide a new idea that further supports the
main theme found in the chorus. The bridge can also
be musical in nature, omitting lyrics and using the
section for an instrumental solo.

As a rule of thumb, contemporary music is composed in eight-bar sections. In other words, the verse
and chorus should each consist of eight bars of
music. However, once again, this eight-bar section is
suggested only as a guideline. There are wonderful
songs with eight-bar verses and four-bar choruses.
The length of a section doesn't have to be either eight
bars or four bars in length. For example, a verse

might be more effective with a musical figure that adds a bar or two and builds nicely to the chorus. Or the theme in the chorus might be better emphasized if the last line is repeated once or twice, adding to the original eight bars.

Worship songs especially seem to lend themselves to varying section lengths. In the song "Never Gonna Stop," the melody line of the chorus is eight bars long, but that eight-bar section is always sung twice, each time with a different lyric.

> *So I'm never gonna stop, never gonna stop*
> *Lifting up my hands to You, lifting up my heart.*
> *When the last day comes and goes and time will be*
>   *no more*
> *I'll be praising You.* [8 bars][14]

The bridge of "Lift Up Your Heads" is structured in the same way. The melody line of the chorus consists of eight bars of music that is repeated twice. The lyric is slightly different for each eight-bar section.

> *Who is this King of glory*
> *Lord of pow'r*
> *His name is Jesus, our risen King* [8 bars]

Who is this King so mighty
Lord of strength
His name is Jesus, our risen King [8 bars][15]

Chord Progressions

If you are a beginning songwriter, try playing one of these simple chord progressions. These are called 1, 4, 5 progressions, because they utilize the first, fourth and fifth chords in a major chord scale:

C, F, G
D, G, A
E, A, B
F, Bb, C
G, C, D

After you become familiar with the 1, 4, 5 progressions, try adding relative minor chords. Relative minor chords are chords found three half-steps or a minor third below the related major 1, 4, 5 chords that I referenced above:

The relative minor of C is A minor.
The relative minor of F is D minor.
The relative minor of G is E minor.

Once you learn both the major chords and their relative minors, you'll have six chords to choose from instead of just three.

Here is an example of chord progression in the key of C:

C, Am, F, Dm, G, Em

This same principle works in any key. Let's try the key of E this time:

The relative minor of E is C# minor.
The relative minor of A is F# minor.
The relative minor of B is G# minor.

The combined major and minor progression is

E - C#m - A - F#m - B - G#m

Rhythm

Rhythm plays a huge role in my writing. It is especially helpful when creating a sense of variety and freshness. Here are some of the most commonly used rhythms, with song examples to illustrate them:

Shuffle—"Amen"
Country/Rock—"He Saved Us to Show His Glory"
6/8 Gospel—"Ah, Lord God"
Latin—"Te Alabamos"
Reggae—"How I Love You, Lord"

Although many songwriters allow the majority of their songs to end up at similar tempos and in a 4/4 time signature, this is a very limiting approach to writing. After all, there is a whole world of rhythms and grooves out there just waiting to be used.

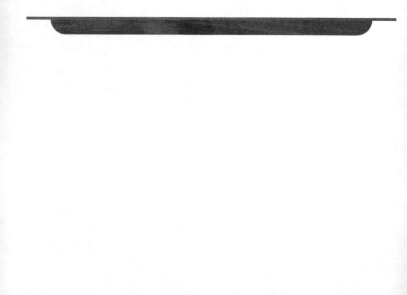

chapter 7

The Songwriter's Toolbox

Here are some tools that can help you make songwriting a lifestyle.

Portable Recorder

I already mentioned the role that my portable digital recorder plays in my songwriting process. I keep my recorder with me at all times. I can talk, sing or play into it. When a song gets close to being finished, I can record the whole song into my recorder, plug it into the speakers in my studio (the studio is not a necessity), and play it all back. Since ideas can materialize at any time, I urge you to use a similar device.

Computers and Software

A computer is a powerful tool for any songwriter. Only a few years ago you would have to go to a professional recording studio and pay a hefty hourly rate to get a high-quality recording. Today, digital audio and MIDI (Musical Instrument Digital Interface—an internationally accepted protocol that allows musically related data to be conveyed from one device to another) software has made it possible to produce professional quality recordings from your living room.

Of course, you can use recording software for more than just creating a polished CD. I use my software simply to try out different ideas. For instance, I might want to see how a drum groove sounds on a particular chorus. It might influence how I end up writing a melody line or a lyrical phrase. I might want to drop in a string part to see if it changes the emotional impact of the song. The experimental possibilities are virtually endless.

Notation software is also available to songwriters. Allegro®, Finale®, and Overture® are just a few popular applications. I use software called Encore®. I always make lead sheets (a notated melody line with chord symbols and lyrics) of my finished songs. Lead sheets are extremely helpful for teaching new songs to my worship team. I have also found that it helps to chart out the notes to the melody, because this forces me to be more rhythmically consistent. Consistency in the rhythm is very helpful when leading a congregation in singing. It also enables the people on the worship team to be more precise when they are teaching it to each other as well as to the congregation.

I also use my computer to house lengthy files of ideas for lyrics. I divide the files into different song categories: Scripture, missions, discipleship, revival, repentance, and so on. If I begin working on an idea but for some reason can't finish it, I file it. Later, when I have a new melody but no lyrics, I'll refer to my files. Quite often I'll also get a new lyric idea, then take ideas from one of those files that contains unfinished lyrics. The combination gets me to a new, completed song.

Recording Hardware

Today's technology makes it possible to buy a four-track cassette recorder for about $150, and you don't have to be a trained engineer to operate it. If you feel more comfortable working with an actual piece of hardware, as opposed to computer software, this can be a good and economical way to record your songs.

Another helpful piece of gear is the drum machine. Drum machines can help you discover new rhythms and inspire you to try new approaches to your songs. Drum machines are also a necessity when it comes to producing demo recordings.

Reference Books

Reference books are a great way to trigger new ideas or inspire alternate approaches to a song that you're working on. Here are just a few that I use and recommend:

Bible (take the time to read different versions)
Bible commentaries
Concordances and other Bible study materials
Thesaurus
Dictionary
Rhyming dictionary

You can find those reference materials in any well-stocked bookstore or library. Of course, if you want a better selection of Bibles or Bible commentaries, a Christian bookstore is the place to go.

chapter 8

The Business of Music

The business of music is another topic on which entire books have been written, but I'd like to offer a few of my personal thoughts on this subject and provide some basic guidelines.

MOTIVES

Several years ago, a Christian record company asked me to write a song with a particular theme for a recording project. If they accepted the song, it would mean a substantial amount of writing royalties down the road. After giving the proposal some thought, I concluded that it was a great opportunity. I accepted the job and wrote the song. Suddenly, for the first time in my life, I found myself in the worship business. Talk about two words that don't seem to go together! Up to that point, I had only written songs for the Lord and for my church. Now, I felt challenged in my spirit, because I realized that I could use this God-given gift for personal gain.

The song turned out okay, but it didn't actually become part of the recording that it was commissioned for. The same record company eventually accepted the song for a different project the following year.

A few years later—the year 2000 to be exact—I was experiencing a lot of stress and a sense of hurriedness (this was the year when we all thought our computers were going to crash at the turn of the millennium!). I was only weeks away from recording my first live worship CD with Integrity, and, to be honest, I was nervous about making a good first impression on everyone I was working with. In other words, in the midst of making a worship recording, I started doing everything except worship. The next thing I knew, I was in my office alone, crying out to God and telling Him that I didn't want earthly success or cool arrangements, but just the touch of His loving hand. To express that thought, I wrote the song "When All Is Said and Done" and these words "All that I long for, all that I hope for is just that sense of You coming near."

Because of various opportunities that God has so graciously given to me, I find that I must constantly check my heart to keep my writing as pure and authentic as possible. The million-dollar question that every songwriter must ask himself or herself is, How do I keep my motives pure? We all battle with a longing for personal glory and financial gain. How does a person keep from giving in to that longing? One thing I can tell you for sure: Entering God's presence is the most effective way to keep your focus in the right place.

Hebrews 10:22 admonishes us to "draw near to God with a sincere heart in full assurance of faith, having our hearts sprinkled to cleanse us from a guilty conscience and having our bodies washed with pure water." When I draw near to God, I am always reminded of where to find real joy and fulfillment. I instantly realize how small I am and how great He is. I'm reminded that He is the *only* One created for, and deserving of, glory.

In Psalm 73, the psalmist admits his envy over the prosperity of the wicked. "When I tried to understand all this, it was oppressive to me till I entered the sanctuary of God; then I understood their final destiny." How simple can it be? For me, running directly to God's presence and worshiping is what sets my motives straight every time. It all comes down to the belief that we should ultimately write songs for God Himself. He is, first and foremost, our audience. How can we go wrong if we keep God the focus of our creativity?

GETTING YOUR SONGS OUT THERE

Even though commercial success can be gratifying, I believe that most creative people who pursue their art for the sake of financial or material rewards end up leading unfulfilled and even unhappy lives. This is especially true for the writer of worship songs. Your first goal should be to create a song that glorifies God; anything beyond that is icing on the cake. With that caveat, the following is some basic information regarding how you can get your songs heard by the music industry.

Your Church
If possible, performing your songs in front of the congregation at your church can be an excellent way

for you to get your songs heard. This is something that has worked well for me as a worship leader.

I believe that writers of worship songs should write for their local churches, not for the Christian music industry. The reason for this is because the Christian music industry should always be tuned in to what the people in local churches are asking for. The industry is supposed to keep its finger on the pulse of the Church. If your song is good and gains popularity at one church, chances are it won't be long before other churches and church groups will begin to use it.

Record companies want a good song with a proven track record. All of my most widely recorded songs were first sung in my church and in several other churches before ever being recorded. In my experience, attempting to force open music industry doors rarely works. Persistence is certainly important, but the key is to be faithful within your own circles of influence. Do your preparation work, develop your craft and be ready when the doors eventually open.

Church Worship Recordings

If you and other songwriters at your church compose enough quality worship songs, your church may decide to record a church worship CD. A church CD recording project can be a wonderful thing. It can build unity and momentum among your worship team and push you toward excellence. A church CD is also a positive experience for the entire congregation because it is a tangible representation of the congregation's own expression of worship.

Here are a few basic tips about creating a church worship recording:

- Take your time and commit to doing the best job possible. If your first CD is great, more people will want you to record a second one.
- Hire a professional producer. Make the effort to find a professional who has experience and understands the heartbeat of your ministry, and allow him or her to help guide you through the project.
- Don't be afraid to hire professional musicians to help out, especially if you or other members of your team tend to be weak on certain instruments.
- Be aware that live recordings are much more difficult to produce than studio recordings.

Studio recordings provide an environment of control and allow you to experiment. If someone makes a mistake, you can easily correct it on the spot. For a live recording, however, you are often recording in a room packed with people, so there will be more variables beyond your control. The performance must be impeccable; if anyone makes a mistake, it must be a mistake that is small enough to fix during postproduction.

- Make sure the drummer plays to a click track. Drums often lay the foundation for a song. If they're not solid, the entire foundation for the song is weak. A click track assures that the meter of your song will remain consistent, which will make the process of fixing mistakes or making adjustments in postproduction easier.

- Make sure all the songs you intend to record are good ones. One of the best ways to determine the quality of a song is to simply pay attention to the response that it gets from your congregation during worship. No record company or A and R person can determine the success of a song as well as a worshiping congregation. Don't be overly anxious and rush into the recording process if some of the songs don't reflect the quality you are seeking. Wait until you've written a few more great songs, or find a well-known favorite and record your own version of the song.

Song Demos

If you plan to submit an original song to a music publisher or record company, a demo recording is an absolute necessity. I want to emphasize, however, that it should be a proven, great song—the greatest producers in the world can only do so much for a mediocre song.

Make sure the quality of your demo recording is first-rate. In a perfect world, record company representatives, artists, producers and publishers put your CD or tape into their player, lean back, close their eyes and listen to your entire song without any interruptions. In the real world, however, you will be lucky if they listen to one complete verse and chorus. You have, at most, about 30 seconds to capture the listener's attention. A high-quality recording plays an important part in accomplishing this.

Send only one song at a time. If you have more then one song that you strongly believe in, send each song separately and at different times. Since you are trying to influence an extremely busy person who probably receives hundreds of recordings every week, he or she will appreciate your professionalism in sending just one tune to consider. If the person likes the one song you send but can't use it at that time, your single song may serve to whet his or her appetite and make that music company representative interested in hearing more of your work at a later time.

CDs seem to be the preferred method for submitting demos, but most music industry folks will also accept a cassette tape. Send a lead sheet with your recording or, at the very least, a lyric sheet.

Look Professional, Be Professional

Address your submission properly and professionally. Correctly spell the company name and the name of the person to whom you're submitting your song. Print the information on the envelope neatly or use a typed or computer-generated label. Make sure that your name, the name of your church or ministry (if applicable) and your address and telephone number appear on the recording package, as well as on the recording label and your cover letter. Your cover letter should be short and to the point. Remember that you're dealing with busy people. They don't want to read the history of how you wrote the song, your personal story or what you hope to be when you grow up in the worship music industry. A short, concise letter labels you as a professional who respects the record company representative's time limitations.

It's best if you're not perceived as a lone ranger. Personal referrals are the best way to get your foot in the door when you're first starting out. If you can get to know someone in the company to whom you want to submit a song, or someone who has an established relationship with the company, it can be a great help. Your contact can submit the song for you and provide you with a credibility that you wouldn't have if you approached the company on your own. Even submitting your song using the name of your church or your church worship department can provide you with added credibility.

Rejection is a part of the creative process. You will undoubtedly experience at least some rejection as you begin to get your songs out into the world. Don't let this stop you. Some big, important record or publishing company might reject your song, but if that song provides a glimpse of God's truth to even a single person, you've already succeeded in a powerful way.

Protecting Your Songs—the Copyright

If you plan to circulate recordings of your songs, perform your original songs publicly, or otherwise make them available to the public, it is a good idea to protect the ownership of your work. The best way to safeguard an original song is to obtain a copyright. Copyright registration is a form of protection provided by the laws of the United States to the authors of original works of authorship. This protection is available to both published and unpublished works (other countries have similar procedures).

Most people do not realize that a copyright is secured automatically when a work (in this case, a song) is created. The copyright office recognizes a song as having been created when it is established in a copy for the first time—for example, the first time you write out a lead sheet or make a recording. So it's not absolutely necessary to register a song; the copyright office recognizes your ownership without that paperwork.

However, there are definite advantages to going through the registration process and paying the fee to secure copyright for your song. First and foremost, copyright registration creates a public record of the copyright claim and legally establishes that you are the primary and original owner of the song. Should someone attempt to use your song illegally, a copyright registration will allow you to file an infringement suit in court.

Obtaining a copyright is a simple process that consists of completing a two-page form, paying a registration fee (currently $30) and mailing either a lead sheet or a recording of your song to the Copyright Office of the Library of Congress. Since obtaining a copyrighting on every song that you write can get expensive, try to choose only the songs that you believe in most strongly—that you believe have the most potential—and protect just those songs. Your song will be protected from the moment it is created, through your lifetime, plus 70 years. In the case of a song written by collaboration, the term lasts for 70 years after the last surviving author's death.

The proper copyright form to register a song or song recording is the Performing Arts (PA) form. It can be obtained by writing to:

Library of Congress
Copyright Office
101 Independence Avenue, S.E.
Washington, D.C. 20559-6000

You can also download forms and learn almost everything you need to know about copyright laws at the following website:

www.loc.gov/copyright

You should note that copyright office fees are subject to change. The website is a great way to make sure that you are up to date on this kind of information.

To register a copyright, mail the following items to the copyright office in a single envelope:

1. A properly completed application form.
2. A nonrefundable filing fee of $30 (or the current rate) for each application.
3. A nonreturnable deposit of the work being registered—in other words, a lead sheet or recording of the song being copyrighted.

The deposit requirements vary in particular situations. Copyright forms contain detailed instructions, so read them carefully to avoid mistakes and complications.

Music Publishing

There are four main sources of income for a songwriter: sheet music, mechanical royalties, performance royalties and foreign publishing. Here's a brief breakdown of what is involved with each of these sources:

- Sheet Music—A song generally has to be recorded, widely distributed and well known to merit having sheet music printed.
- Mechanical Royalties—Mechanical royalties come from the sales of CDs, cassette tapes, videotapes, piano rolls or the newer digital piano disks and video or DVD disks. In other words, any medium that produces a recording of a song should generate income for the writer. At the time of this writing, there is great controversy in the music industry about how to monitor and collect royalties from internet sources of distribution such as mp3 music files.
- Performance Royalties—If a song is performed on the radio, television, jukeboxes or in auditoriums, churches or sports arenas, the writer receives performance royalties.

Once a songwriter is published, he or she must join one of the following organizations: ASCAP (American Society of Composers, Authors and Publishers), BMI (Broadcast Music, Inc.) or SESAC (Society of European Stage Authors and Composers). These organizations monitor the performance, collect fees and distribute royalties on behalf of their members. Christian music performed in churches is licensed by CCLI (Christian Copyright Licensing International).

- Foreign Royalties—In this world of technology and instant communication, music is easily distributed all over the world. An American publisher might be large enough to have branch offices around the world. If a publisher isn't international, it can license music to foreign publishers in order to generate sales and collect royalties in foreign territories.

As the creator of the product in question, the songwriter receives at least 50 percent of all income in a music publishing deal. As long as a song is copyrighted, it is against the law for the publishing company to pay the songwriter any less then half of the income it receives for the song. Note that I state "at least 50 percent": Once a songwriter has songs that are well known in hundreds of churches and radio stations and by countless performers, he or she has the leverage to ask for a co-publishing deal. As the name suggests, in a co-publishing deal, the songwriter receives a percentage of the publisher's 50 percent in addition to the 50 percent writing royalty.

Why would publishers want to give a percentage of their half of the money to the songwriter? It's simple: The fact that a particular songwriter's songs are widely known and played is a barometer of the popularity of the songs. This popularity is a strong indication that future songs from the same songwriter will do just as well. It's more of a "sure thing" for the publisher. A publisher will be willing to share a little more of the profit to prevent the songwriter from going to another publisher.

If you're a somewhat unknown writer, there are several reasons why you shouldn't fight for a copublishing deal. First, if you come across as a fighter too early in your career, the publishing company will label you as difficult to work with and gladly move on.

After all, the world is full of talented songwriters. Second, it's the publisher's job to get your song into the marketplace and make your song known. If you're relatively unknown and your song is unknown, the publisher has a rough job ahead and deserves all of the 50 percent publishing income. If the publisher does a good job and your songs become well known, widely used in churches and widely recorded, more of a partnership will have been created. At that point you can think about negotiating a better deal.

Many new or inexperienced songwriters are fearful of having their songs stolen by music publishers. I know people who are so protective of their songs that the songs never end up being heard, let alone published. That seems rather silly to me when you consider that half of something (a 50 percent writer's royalty, for instance) is a lot more than 100 percent of nothing.

It's important to realize that music publishers are generally honest, smart people. They aren't going to bite the hand that feeds them. Granted, they are in the music business, which means they need to make a profit; but they know that in the long run, it will not pay them to steal songs. If word were to spread that a publisher was stealing songs, it wouldn't be long before all songwriters would stop doing any business with that publisher. So don't be afraid—just get those songs out there!

chapter 9

A Songwriter's Lifestyle

I love the competition in sports and I would enjoy getting my exercise consistently by playing basketball or tennis. However, I've found that I've had to stick to exercise routines that don't require anybody else's help or participation. In today's busy world it's often difficult to schedule a single tennis partner, let alone find enough people for a basketball team who are all available at the same time. If I waited to exercise until I could find enough people who would play that basketball game, I'd rarely get any exercise at all.

Songwriting can be like exercising. I know several people who are musically inclined and have plenty of ideas for songs, but since they don't play an instrument, their songwriting is heavily dependent on the skill of musicians who can play an instrument.

If there is any way that you can learn even a few chords on the guitar or piano, you won't have to depend on anyone else. Obviously this isn't always a necessity, especially if you're collaborating by choice. Some collaborations can be wonderful and very productive. But I have found it to be a huge blessing to be able to both write and play music.

Many of the greatest worship songs of all time consist of just three chords. Keys can be changed and other musicians can embellish chord progressions later. Give it a try! Take a music lesson and learn to play a simple song. You'll be surprised how those three or four chords can later be turned into songs of your own.

Change Instruments

When I'm in a songwriting rut, I often will sit down at the piano. I'm primarily a guitarist and I can only play a few chords on any other instrument, so approaching the songwriting process with an instrument other than my guitar, the instrument I'm most comfortable with, forces me to approach songwriting from a different perspective.

How Much Music Theory?

I encourage new songwriters to get as much musical

theory education as possible. The more you know about music—the more instruments you know how to play and the more musical styles you become acquainted with—the greater your ability will be to write great worship songs. If you study, work hard at your music, really apply yourself and have some ability, you'll be ready when inspiration hits.

I once met a man who told me he didn't want to learn any music theory because it would stifle his creativity. The entire time he was explaining his reasons for this decision, I was fairly certain that it was only his own laziness that was really stopping him from getting a better musical education. I assured him that once he knew all the rules, he would be free to break them.

Before you get discouraged, let me assure you that I'm not suggesting that you enroll as a music major at the nearest college. Actually, you don't have to know as much as you might think. Some of the really great songwriters don't even read music. I find it interesting that some people, many times classical musicians, seem to be gifted in being able to read and perform a piece of music with exact perfection every time. Other musicians can't play a simple piece the same way twice, but have a gift for creating new music. That's where songwriters come in, and that's why they don't have to be extensively educated in the field of music. If you have the creative gift, thank God for it every day. There are plenty of musicians out there who can perform your song to perfection after you've written it.

If you're not sure exactly where you should begin your music theory education, you might want to start with chord theory. My formal musical education is an accumulated total of about one full year of music school plus an additional six months of private guitar lessons. I learned a great deal of chord theory as well as extensive study in different chord progressions. Chord theory has helped me to learn a variety of different voicings (ranges) for each chord. It's amazing how just playing the same chord a different way or with a different voicing will spark a melodic idea.

The study of chord progressions enabled me to learn all the possible chords that can be played in a given key. This can be compared to an artist acquiring a larger palette of colors for a painting. Since worship songs require simple, singable melodies, it is very helpful to know a greater variety of chords and progressions. The worship songwriter can use this broader variety of chords to create musical interest underneath a simple melody.

Worship songs can easily end up sounding predictable. I try to avoid predictability by experimenting with different chords and progressions, no matter how simple the melody line. My song "How Lovely Your Dwelling Place" is a good example. There are a fair amount of chords in this song, but the melody is very simple.

Stay Open to Suggestions

Proverbs 19:20, tells us, "Listen to advice and accept instruction, and in the end you will be wise." I remember a man telling me at Bible school that his song could not be altered in any way because God gave him the song just the way it was. Had God really spoken to this songwriter, or was he just too insecure or full of pride to accept any feedback? I won't claim to know this man's heart, but I do know that few songs emerge from our songwriting reservoir absolutely perfect. There are some exceptions, but it's very rare.

Keep in mind that songwriting is simply an art form, and art is all about creative possibilities. It's extremely important that you have trusted people in your life who can provide you with constructive, honest feedback. Sometimes a simple, objective suggestion can make a big difference in a new song.

It won't always be easy to be open and nondefensive about your songs. When my songs first began to be recorded by other artists, invariably the arranger would make a slight change just so that the recording would have his unique touch. Without fail, I'd hate the change. Eventually though, I began to realize that it wasn't really a big deal. There was nothing I could do about it, anyway.

I've now reached the place where I can actually be entertained (I mean that in the most positive way) by how someone else interprets a worship song that came from my heart. There have even been times when a producer put a new spin on one of my songs and I ended up enjoying it more than when I originally wrote it.

I'm only trying to caution you to be careful that you don't over spiritualize how a song is birthed. Some songs are written in minutes, some take months. In the end, it's all about a gifting and a calling that God has given you. It's not so much about the song itself, it's about what God does through it.

Rewrites

I've heard it said that great songs aren't written, they're rewritten. That may or may not be true, but I think it's possible to rewrite a song too many times. You need to be careful about overworking a song that you perceive to be a problem. This is especially true if you find yourself in a writing slump. It just may be that the song in question doesn't need a rewrite, you just need to get those creative juices flowing again.

There comes a point when it's better to have one imperfect, completed song in your files than an entire collection of forgotten, unfinished songs. You may also find that there are many times when your imperfect songs are actually better then you think. Once again, this is when you really need someone else's ear. It's easy for us creative types to get worked up or overly concerned about something insignificant in our song—something that looks big to us but doesn't really matter. Someone else's perspective can help to restore objectivity.

Sometimes you may write a song and think that you're finished, but suddenly receive inspiration that leads to a rewrite. The story of my song "These Things Are True of You" is a rewrite of sorts. To ponder the attributes of God is a very worshipful exercise for me, and I wanted to write a song about who He is. I wanted the music to sound a little bit like a hymn, because the lyrics were coming out in a hymn style with lots of theology. I wrote the verses, and just like we find in many hymns, it had no chorus. Even so, I thought I was done. I thought it was pretty good and I really liked the hook—"make these things true of me too." So there I was, living in the moment and being blessed as I sang it, when suddenly I thought, *Wow, God, You are so wonderful and awesome, I want to be just like You!* You see, that's what happens whenever you worship something—you want to become just like it. So I knew there would have to be a chorus with the line "make these things true of me too."

Songwriting Is Spelled W-O-R-K

A songwriter's biggest enemy is his or her unfinished songs. We either get tired and lazy, or we get discouraged with how a song is turning out. We don't like the direction the writing is heading or we're convinced the song isn't as good as our last one. So what do we do? We give up.

This has certainly happened to me, but I have found that not giving up too soon enables me to create a flow. It's similar to when you first turn on a hot water faucet. At first the water flows out cold. It takes a while for the water to get hot. Once the water is hot, you can turn the faucet off and turn it on again and the hot water will come out hot right away.

Songwriting works in much the same way. It often takes a while for the really hot ideas to begin flowing. Force yourself to finish those songs that are giving you trouble—those songs that you don't have 100 percent confidence in. You may be surprised at how quickly the cold ideas turn to hot. Some of my best songs are the ones I originally gave up on but had the discipline to eventually finish.

Persistence

When my publisher told me that they would like to release a new version of this book, which was originally published by my church, I thought it would be inspiring to add more song stories and extra thoughts. I had worked numerous hours on this project and was nearly done, when my computer was stolen. I lost everything I had written. Not only that, I also lost several of my latest songs and song ideas. I was devastated and learned a valuable lesson about backing up my work. As I grieved my loss, I heard the Lord remind me of something: *It's not what was in your computer that's important, it's what I've placed in you that's important.* My relationship with God and the gifting He has given me to communicate that relationship to the world is a priceless gift and can never be taken away from me. No thief can steal it and no discouraging words or disappointing situations can take it away. It is Jesus in me!

Because of this truth, I can choose to believe that the words I'm writing to you now are the words that were meant for this book. Though I lost some songs in this process, I know that God will give me new ones. Just like when my songs bomb or get rejected, I say to myself, *Tommy, just write another one.*

To state this another way, you may have filled up your bathtub with water only to have it drain out just when you were getting ready to get in. Although it may be frustrating, all you have to do is turn on the faucet again and fill up the tub. The most important thing is that the faucet is ready to be turned on again. No matter what, the source is the important thing, and the source is living in you. His name is Emmanuel—God with us!

Creative people who have experienced ongoing success have tough skin. In most cases they weren't successful overnight. They experienced a lot of rejection and a lot of discouragement. But they were persistent. They stayed with it.

Some of the most gifted people I know have never reached their potential because they are too afraid of rejection. A friend of mine who experienced rejection when presenting a song to a band told me later that he vowed to never try again. I felt that this person had a more natural gift for songwriting than I did. He just wasn't willing to take the risk. My friend could have written songs that would have literally saved lives, but he gave up too soon because of fear, pride and self-concern.

As a teenager, I played in a Christian band. I remember writing a song that I was convinced was absolutely awesome. I just loved it. The guys in the band were all my best friends, so I sang the entire song for them. Every one of them almost died laughing, rolling on the floor, and told me it was the most stupid song they'd ever heard. I was crushed. Somehow, by His grace, God enabled me to keep trying.

All artists risk rejection. Songwriting feels like one of the most risky of all art forms, because a good song will require that you pour so much of yourself into it. Let me assure you that it is worth the risk. It is worth the times of failure. A well-known motivational speaker has said that if you try your best and learn something along the way, you have truly succeeded.

Making Time

Writing a song is rarely a necessity, and few people are fortunate enough to earn a good living as a songwriter. Because of this, you will probably find that songwriting gets moved down the list behind studying for a test, buying groceries, going to your child's school play or just earning a living.

Songwriting does not happen by accident. You have to develop discipline and purposefulness to keep writing. One of my better-known songs, "He Knows My Name," was written from nothing more than sheer discipline. My pastor had written a sermon with this title and asked me to write a song to go with the sermon. I wasn't inspired in any way. The song really didn't excite me as it developed and took form. I only wrote it because writing worship songs for my church is part of my job description.

If I hadn't put aside the time and finished what I originally thought was a very mediocre song, "He Knows My Name" wouldn't exist today. I would have missed an opportunity to see God use one of my simple songs in a profound way. I've seen thousands of people come to Christ while singing this song at Promise Keepers and Harvest Crusade events, as well as during foreign mission concert tours. I encourage you with all my heart to take the time and make the time to write. You never know the eternal significance that could come out of a song you have yet to create.

If you're not naturally disciplined, then you might try the assigned-time technique to develop this quality. I mentioned earlier that many creative people have a specific time of day or night when they are the most productive. That particular time of day will work best with this technique. If you don't know when you are most creative, or if you're simply not available at that particular time of day to write songs, you can still effectively use this technique to develop discipline.

Here is how it works. Choose a specific time during the day (or night) when you know you're free to apply yourself to songwriting. Commit to a specific amount of time that you will spend doing just that. Start out with a short period of time, such as 15 minutes or so. Most of us can stay in one place, doing one thing, for 15 minutes.

Next, commit to not doing anything else for that 15-minute time period. Even if you sit in your chair staring at a blank sheet of paper, do nothing else except think about the song you're working on. Don't read

your mail. Don't switch on the television. Don't pro-
gram the next best-selling computer game. Just focus
on songwriting.

The first day, you may write a word or two or a
note or two. You may write nothing at all. It doesn't
matter as long as you stay with it for 15 minutes. The
next day may produce the same results, and the next
day the same thing. Eventually you'll find that your
15 minutes ends with some progress showing up on
paper or on your tape recorder.

Once you feel like it's easy staying with it for 15
minutes, bump your assigned time for songwriting up
to 30 minutes. When you feel like you can handle 45
minutes, go for it. Before you know it, you'll be spending two or three hours at a time as a songwriter.

Being Obedient

I had just finished leading a Promise Keepers event
that took place on the east coast. As I left the stadi-
um, I found myself on a huge high but completely
exhausted from all the excitement. I couldn't wait to
get to my hotel room to rest. When I finally did get
to my room the realization that I was away from
home and alone hit me pretty hard. I also realized
that I had a television set in my room with quite a

few channels that I had no business watching.

Sometimes we're the most vulnerable when we're coming down from an emotional high and are tired. And of course, the forces of the Enemy are always looking for an opportunity to mess with our lives. I must confess that I wanted to turn that television on. I struggled with the temptation. Finally, I got to a point where I said, *Lord, after all You've done for me, I'm not going to do this.* So I committed myself to not even switch on the TV for the entire night.

It was only eight o'clock in the evening. I was on Pacific Standard Time—three hours earlier—so I knew that I was going to be awake until two o'clock in the morning. I was alone. I didn't have a car. I didn't even have an acoustic guitar with me. Basically, I had nothing to do but sit on my hotel room bed and not watch TV.

It didn't take too long for me to pick up my electric guitar and start strumming it. All of a sudden, it was as if God said, "Well, here's your gift." The words came, and I heard "That's why we praise Him, that's why we sing . . ." I grabbed a piece of paper and started writing. This was one time when I knew a song was really going to touch a lot of people. It's as if God was saying, "See what I can do with a little act of obedience?" Not only did I sleep that night in total peace with a sense of having loved and honored God, but multitudes of people have since been led to His throne because one guy (me) said yes to obeying God. "That's Why We Praise Him" is featured on the WOW Green CD, Promise Keepers' "Go The Distance" CD, Song Discovery Volume 17, and Christian Assembly's "Live at Home" double CD. What a gracious rewarder our God is! To Him be all the Glory!

chapter 10

Parting Words

When my first few songs were being recorded, I was completely caught up by the power that certain people appeared to hold. I had been writing songs since I was 11 years old and had worked hard to succeed. Then in a heartbeat, some man in a record company held the power to make my dream come true—or not.

Back then, every opportunity seemed to me as if it would be my one shot at success. I allowed myself to be controlled by what the people in the music industry thought of me. If they liked me, I believed I was worth something. If they didn't like me, I felt worthless.

Now that I've worked and worshiped in the music world for several years, I see that it was always only God who called and appointed me. It was God who gave me this songwriting ability and ultimately it was He who provided every opportunity along the way. No human being in the music industry did it. God did it.

I also know now that it was never just one shot. God had many more songs to give me. He had—and has—many more opportunities to give me. It was all about me being faithful, one song at a time. It was about being prepared when the opportunities actually presented themselves.

I mentioned earlier that songwriting is a lifestyle for me. I plan on digging in and writing worship songs for the rest of my life. If the song I'm currently working on doesn't come together or gets rejected, I'll just write another one. Ultimately, what I will cherish most are those times when I felt God's smile. I will take joy in those moments when I felt that I wrote a song that truly helped just one person, sitting at the end of the second row in my church, connect with God. Somewhere in the midst of the struggle that is songwriting is a fulfillment no worldly success can ever provide. Notoriety and money can be great blessings, but nothing compares to the holy moments I've shared with the Lord as I sensed Him plant a lyric or melody in my heart—as He whispered what He knew my soul was longing to say to Him.

Remember that God your Father loves every worship song that truly comes from your heart. First and foremost, write for Him and to Him, your audience of One. Then you can proceed in the knowledge that you are never wasting your time. If He's the only one that ever hears the song, it is still worth doing. I pray that the inspiration of the Holy Spirit will be upon you as you live this journey of expressing your heart in song. I pray that you learn how to express nothing less than genuine, heartfelt worship to God, and that you help people all over the world to do the same.

God's richest blessings on you,

Tommy

1. Tommy Walker, "There Is a Rock," © 2002 WeMobile Music/BMI.
2. Tommy Walker, "What a Good God," © 1987 Mercy Publishing.
3. Tommy Walker, "Lord, I Run to You," © 2004 Integrity Music.
4. Tommy Walker, "Be Still and Know," © 1998 WeMobile Music/BMI/Enchanted Dance.
5. Tommy Walker, "How Good and Pleasant," © 1999 Integrity Music.
6. Tommy Walker, "He Knows My Name," © 1996 WeMobile Music.
7. Tommy Walker, "Everyone Arise," © 1999 WeMobile Music.
8. Tommy Walker, "That's Why We Praise Him," © 1998 WeMobile Music/Doulos/BMI.
9. Tommy Walker, "Let's Think About Our God," © 2000 Integrity Music.
10. Tommy Walker, "Only a God Like You," © 2000 Integrity Music.
11. Tommy Walker, "Lord, I Believe in You," © 1996 Doulos.
12. Tommy Walker, "How Good and Pleasant," © 1999 Integrity Music.
13. Philip B. Bliss, arr. by Tommy Walker, "Hallelujah, What a Savior!" © 2004 Integrity Music.
14. Tommy Walker, "Never Gonna Stop," © 2000 Integrity Music.
15. Tommy Walker, "Lift Up Your Heads," © 1998 Integrity Music.

Calling Out to You— Live Worship

Sweet Presence · Don't Forget His Benefits · Mourning into Dancing · Calling Out to You · Show Your Glory · It Will Be Worth It All · When We See Him · Holy · His Love Endures Forever

Never Gonna Stop

How Good and Pleasant · Only a God Like You · He Saved Us · To Show His Glory · Give Us the Sounds · Jesus, That Name · When All Is Said and Done · I Fix My Eyes on You · Let's Think About Our God · Where You Are · I Hide Myself in Thee · He Knows My Name · How Could I But Love You · Never Gonna Stop

Live at Home

Lift Up Your Heads · Everyone Arise · Joy, Joy, Joy · That's Why We Praise Him · As We Worship You · Come Quickly · Te Albamos · Medley—There's No Greater Love, His Love Endures Forever, Mourning into Dancing, Lord I Believe in You, Do You Know · God Is Near · Be Still and Know · I Know That My Redeemer Lives · Doxology · Unto the King · Amen

Make It Glorious

Prepare Ye the Way • Make It Glorious • Jesus We Celebrate Your Fame • Heavenly Touch • Thank You for Loving Me • Just Worship • This God He Is Our God • I'm Not Ashamed • Lord I Run to You • Dwelling Place • Hallelujah What a Savior • Your Word Will Be the Last Word

Anthology (1991-2002)

There Is a Rock • He Lives • Sweet Presence of Jesus • Don't Forget His Benefits • Revival Down in My Heart • No Greater Love • I Love This Story • There'll Always Be • Great Redeemer • Here I Am Again • Everyone Arise • Show Your Glory • Great I Am • Holy Spirit Song • Mourning into Dancing • Joy, Joy, Joy • His Love Endures Forever • Yes, We All Agree • Thanks Again • No One Like You • Everlasting Arms • Lord, I Believe in You • Ah Lord God • Calling Out to You • It Will Be Worth It All • Pray for Each Other • When We See Him • Come Quickly • That's Why We Praise Him • As We Worship You • Be Still and Know • These Things Are True of You

Heal Our Land— Live from Zambia

Unto the King • From the Sunrise • I'm Not Ashamed • Praise Him (Psalm 150) • I Will Give You Praise [Only You] • Shine On Us • Calling Out to You • Takwaba Uwaba • Sweet Jesus, Come • Lord I Run to You

To listen to excerpts of some of the songs mentioned in this book, go to www.getdownministries.com

Also Available in the Best-Selling Worship Series

The Unquenchable Worshipper
Coming Back to the Heart of Worship
Matt Redman
ISBN 08307.29135

The Heart of Worship Files
Featuring Contributions from Some
of Today's Most Experienced
Lead Worshippers
Matt Redman, General Editor
ISBN 08307.32616

Here I Am to Worship
Never Lose the Wonder
of Worshiping the Savior
Tim Hughes
ISBN 08307.33221

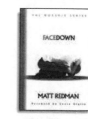

Facedown
When You Face Up to God's Glory, You
Find Yourself Facedown in Worship
Matt Redman
ISBN 08307.32462

Also Available in the Best-Selling Worship Series

Inside, Out Worship
Insights for Passionate and
Purposeful Worship
Matt Redman and *Friends*
ISBN 08307.37103

For the Audience of One
Worshiping the One and Only
in Everything You Do
Mike Pilavachi
ISBN 08307.37049

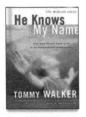

He Knows My Name
How God Knows Each of Us in
an Unspeakably Intimate Way
Tommy Walker
ISBN 08307.36360

The Worship God Is Seeking
An Exploration of Worship
and the Kingdom of God
David Ruis
ISBN 08307.36921